D1069641

The Little Book of
Sign Language

The Little Book of
Sign Language

RUNNING PRESS
PHILADELPHIA • LONDON

A Running Press® Miniature Edition™
©2000 by Running Press
All rights reserved under the Pan-American and
International Copyright Conventions
Printed in China

*This book may not be reproduced in whole or in part,
in any form or by any means, electronic or mechanical,
including photocopying, recording, or by any information
storage and retrieval system now known or hereafter
invented, without written permission from the publisher.*

*The proprietary trade dress, including the size and format,
of this Running Press® Miniature Edition™ is the property
of Running Press. It may not be used or reproduced without
the express written permission of Running Press.*

Library of Congress Cataloging-in-Publication Number
99-75087

ISBN 0-7624-0706-9

This book may be ordered by mail from the publisher.
Please include $1.00 for postage and handling.
But try your bookstore first!

Running Press Book Publishers
125 South Twenty-second Street
Philadelphia, Pennsylvania 19103-4399

Visit us on the web!
www.runningpress.com

contents

introduction   **7**

the alphabet   **13**

the numbers   **23**

greetings and salutations   **29**

family ties   **47**

feelings and emotions   **63**

favorite animals   **81**

favorite foods   **101**

where to learn more   **117**

introduction

In 1694 a Deaf Englishman named Jonathan Lambert moved to Martha's Vineyard with his family of seven children—two of whom were also deaf. From that time on, sign language was common in Martha's Vineyard, and has been part of American life for more than 300 years!

American Sign Language (ASL) is unlike any other language you'll ever study. There are no irregular verbs or dangling participles here. Instead, you'll study the intricacies of eye contact, facial expressions, and body language. It's also important to understand that ASL is not a word-for-word translation of English.

Rather, ASL is a language all its own, just like Spanish, French, and Portuguese.

To many hearing people, sign language is beautiful and fascinating. And that's true. But to Deaf people, sign language is a part of their everyday way of being, and part of their social interactions with friends and families.

Deaf people form their own unique communities in the United States and other countries, and sign language is the glue that binds them together.

As you work through *The Little Book of Sign Language*, you'll learn the basics of communicating in this very special way. We hope you'll enjoy this small glimpse into the

wonderful history and
vibrant culture of Deaf
people in America.

Joseph E. Fischgrund
Headmaster
Pennsylvania School for the Deaf
July 1999

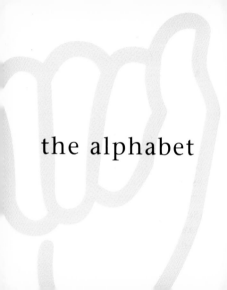

the alphabet

If you're ever unsure of a particular sign, you can "finger spell" it using the American Manual Alphabet. This is often a slow and cumbersome process, but nevertheless useful— especially when telling someone your name (see page 38). You'll also have to finger spell brand names like "Hershey" and

"Kodak," as well as the names of most cities and countries.

These alphabet shapes are the foundations of many signs in ASL. To sign "cheese," for example, you'll use your "C" hand to imitate using a cheese grater (see page 114).

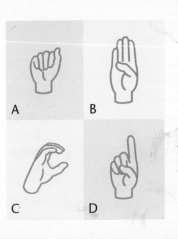

A

B

C

D

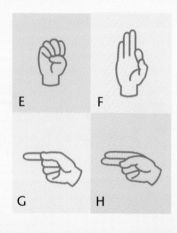

E

F

G

H

I

BELOW:

To sign "J," turn your wrist while drawing a fishhook with your pinkie finger.

J

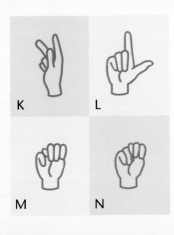

K

L

M

N

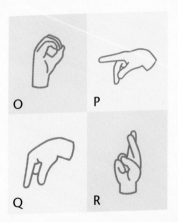

O

P

Q

R

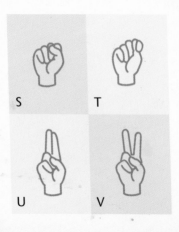

S

T

U

V

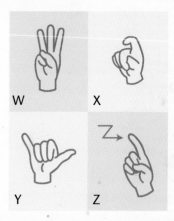

W

X

Y

Z

the numbers

T he handshapes on the following pages will teach you how to sign the numbers one through ten. As with the alphabet, many of these shapes are the foundation for other signs in ASL (particularly #5, which is the open palm shape).

One common mistake made by beginners is to sign #3 by holding up

the middle three fingers.
In ASL, this is actually
the sign for #6! These
signs may seem confusing
at first, but they allow
you to sign ten different
numbers using only
one hand—and how
many hearing people
can do *that*?

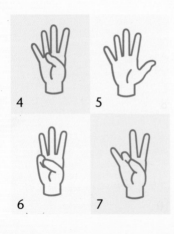

4

5

6

7

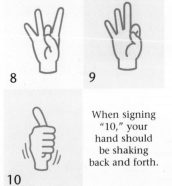

8

9

10

When signing "10," your hand should be shaking back and forth.

greetings
and
salutations

When greeting someone in ASL, the most important thing to remember is eye contact! If you're not watching each other, then you're not "hearing" each other. An appropriate facial expression is also important: if you're signing "I'm sorry" to an upset friend, you shouldn't be smiling!

hello

Beginning with your
fingertips at your
temple, raise the
hand forward in
a casual salute.

excuse me

Brush your fingertips
over your palm in two
short movements.

please

Move your palm in
a circle over the
center of your chest.

what's your name?

ASL: You Name?

To sign *you*, point at the person you are addressing. To sign *name*, extend the middle and index fingers of both hands in an X. Don't forget an inquisitive facial expression!

my name is

ASL: Me Name

To sign *me*, simply
point at yourself.
To sign *name*, extend
the middle and index
fingers of both hands
in an X. You'll have
to finger spell the
letters of your name.

congratulations

Clasp your hands
together and shake
repeatedly.

thank you

Lower your fingertips
from mouth to chest
level. For extra thanks,
use two hands.

goodbye

Raise and lower
your fingers, just like
you're waving goodbye.

family ties

When you compare "male" and "female" signs ("brother" and "sister," "mother" and "father," etc.) you'll notice that the signs are quite similar—except they begin at different parts of the face. In ASL, the upper half of the face is used to describe men, while the lower half is used to describe women.

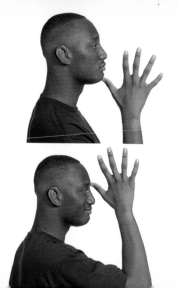

mother

Touch the thumb
of your "5" hand
against the chin.

father

Touch the thumb
of your "5" hand
against the forehead.

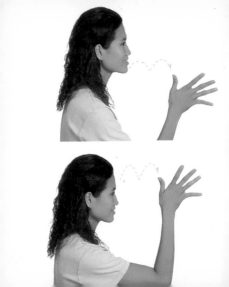

grandmother

Move the "5" hand
away from the chin
in a double arc.

grandfather

Move the "5" hand
away from the forehead
in a double arc.

boy

Pinch the brim of an imaginary baseball cap.

girl

Move your thumb
downward over the
cheek to the chin.

brother

Make the sign for
"boy," then lower
your hand, ending
on the wrist of your
opposite hand.

sister

Make the sign for
"girl," then lower your
hand, ending on
the wrist of your
opposite hand.

baby

Cradle your arms
together and swing
them back and forth.

feelings
and
emotions

Body language is another important aspect of ASL—especially when describing your feelings and emotions. If you're signing the word "tired," try slumping your shoulders. If you're signing "excited," you'll want to move your hands very quickly. In ASL, it's okay to get emotional!

how are you?

ASL: How You?

To sign *how*, begin with
both hands in front of
the chest, palms facing
in and knuckles touch-
ing. Roll the hands
forward, ending with
palms facing up. To sign
you, point at the person
you're addressing.

happy

Brush your hand
upward in a circular
movement over
your chest.

sad

Move both "5" hands
downward from the
eyes, to indicate
falling tears.

tired

Lower your hands
across your chest,
to indicate a drain
of energy through
the body.

flustered

Touch your index
finger to your fore-
head. Then twist wrists
sharply, as if turning
a jar upside-down.

sick

Touch your bent
middle fingers to
your forehead
and stomach.

bored

Keeping the tip of your
index finger against
the nose, twist the
hand forward.

excited

With palms facing you,
move the bent middle
fingers of your hands
in alternating circles.

favorite
animals

I f you've ever wished that you were a cat (or a horse, or even a fish!) then you're bound to enjoy making animal signs in ASL. Many of these signs require you to imitate some aspect of an animal's behavior, so you'll find them very easy to remember.

do you have animals?

ASL: Have Animals?

To sign *have*, touch your fingers to your chest. To sign *animals*, roll your knuckles toward each other with a double movement (to imitate an animal breathing).

dog

Snap your fingers, as
if calling for your
dog's attention.

cat

Move both "F" hands
outward from the
corners of your
mouth (as if pulling
on whiskers).

horse

Bend your fingers up
and down (to indicate
a horse's ears).

fish

Wriggle the hand
forward, like a
fish swimming
downstream.

bird

Open and close your
thumb and index
finger in front of
your "beak."

rabbit

This sign is similar to
"horse," except that
the palms should face
inward, not outward.

favorite
foods

D on't proceed to this next chapter with an empty stomach! Food signs often require us to imitate methods of cooking or eating (to sign hamburger, for example, you'll pretend to shape a meat patty with your hands) so practicing these signs might make you hungry!

what should we eat?

ASL: Eat What?

To sign *eat*, pretend to
hold some imaginary
food near your mouth.
To sign *what*, hold out
your hands and offer a
good shrug. Make sure
you look inquisitive!

hamburger

Clasp one curved palm
over the other; flip
hands and repeat
(like you're shaping
a meat patty).

spaghetti

Raise the pinky fingers
of your "I" hands,
as if lifting pasta
from a plate to
your mouth.

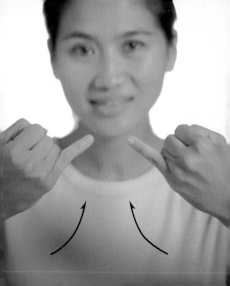

soup

Move your "U" hand
from open palm to
mouth, as if eating
soup from a bowl.

salad

Raise and lower your
open "C" hands, as if
tossing a salad.

hot dog

Trace the outline of hot dog—beginning with open "C" hands and ending with your hands closed in fists.

cheese

Press the heel of your
hand against the palm
of your opposite
hand, as if using
a cheese grater.

where to
learn more

Now that you've finished this book, let's take a moment to review what you've learned. You can sign the complete alphabet and the numbers one through ten. You can finger spell your name. You can greet someone in a conversation, ask how they're doing, and thank them. You can order food in a restaurant. You can even call for your favorite pet spider!

But if you've made it this far, you probably want to learn more about American Sign Language. A good next step would be taking a class with a qualfied ASL instructor. In a classroom setting, you'll meet plenty of students who want to practice ASL. And since most of these students are beginners, you'll feel more confident about your ASL skills as they continue to grow.

On the next four pages, we've listed a number of schools and organizations that offer support to Deaf people and to their families and friends. These places will often send information about ASL and Deaf culture free of charge.

And if you know any Deaf co-workers or acquaintances, don't hesitate to ask them questions about ASL! Most Deaf people have a tremendous respect and enthusiasm for their language, and they're eager to help anyone who's interested in learning more.

Keep signing,
and good luck!

Where to Learn More

If you want to know more about American Sign Language, we recommend that you contact any of the following institutions:

National Association for the Deaf
814 Thayer Avenue
Silver Spring, MD 20910-4500
301-587-1788 (voice)
301-587-1789 (TTY)
website: www.nad.org

National Center on Deafness
California State University, Northridge
18111 Nordhoff Street
Northridge, CA 91330-8267

818-885-2611 V/TTY
818-885-4899 Fax

National Information
Center on Deafness
Gallaudet University
800 Florida Avenue NE
Washington, D.C. 20002
202-651-5051 (voice)
202-651-5052 (TTY)

NTID/RIT Department for ASL
and Interpreting Education
52 Lomb Memorial Drive
Rochester, NY 14623-5604
716-475-6431 V/TTY
716-475-6500 Fax

Registry of Interpreters
for the Deaf, Inc.
511 Monroe Street, Suite 1107
Rockville, MD 20850
301-779-0555 (V/TTY)

Self Help for Hard of Hearing
People, Inc. (SHHH)
7910 Woodmont Avenue,
Suite 1200
Bethesda, MD 20814
301-657-2248 (voice)
301-657-2249 (TTY)
website: www.shhh.org

League for the Hard of Hearing
71 W. 23rd Street
New York, NY 10010
212-741-7650 (voice)
212-255-1932 (TTY)
website: www.lhh.org

The Pennsylvania School
for the Deaf
100 W. School House Lane
Philadelphia, PA 19144
215-951-4700
website: www@psd.org

Modeling Credits

The models in this book are
all Deaf staff members at
The Pennsylvania School
for the Deaf.

Mariton Barrera
Kevin Mundey
Debbie Schanbacher
Bob Shilling
Shirley Simmons

Running Press would like to extend
a special thank-you to Bob Shilling,
our ASL consultant, and to all
of the staff members at the
Pennsylvania School for the Deaf.

This book has been bound
using handcraft methods
and Smyth-sewn to
ensure durability.

The dust jacket and interior
were photographed by
Steven Raniszewski/B.C.P.
and designed by
Terry Peterson.

The text was written by
Jason Rekulak.

The text was set in
Stone Serif and Stone Sans.